EX MACHINA

DATE DUE

Demco, Inc. 38-293

6 2010

Ex Machina

Jonathan Ball

BookThug | Toronto *MMIX*

The production of this book was made possible through the generous
assistance of the Canada Council for the Arts and the Ontario Arts
Council.

 Canada Council **Conseil des Arts**
for the Arts **du Canada**

 ONTARIO ARTS COUNCIL
CONSEIL DES ARTS DE L'ONTARIO

Printed in Canada.

LIBRARY AND ARCHIVES CANADA
CATALOGUING IN PUBLICATION

Ball, Jonathan, 1979-
     Ex machina / Jonathan Ball.

Poems.
ISBN 978-1-897388-48-8

     I. Title.

PS8603.A55E9 2009   C811'.6   C2009-905284-9

[ ] EX MACHINA

[EX MACHINA]

[ ]

Man's very soul is due to the machines; it is a machine-made thing: he thinks as he thinks, and feels as he feels, through the work that machines have wrought upon him, and their existence is quite as much a *sine qua non* for his, as his for theirs.

Samuel Butler, *Erewhon*

This book is a machine.
It will use you to generate poems.

There are numbers.
If you follow these numbers,

then the book may follow you.
Otherwise, the book will continue

without you.

[01]

[02]

The book that you read, seeking something. [60]

The book that you write, to discover. [52]

The book for which they burn you. [35]

The book the bacteria write in your bones. [08]

[03]

Please be aware of these risks. [19]

Do not operate without. [14]

Acknowledge the potential for failure. [18]

When I looked at the sky, I saw clouds forming chains. [63]

[04]

Reconsider your position. [17]

The human above the machine. [40]

The machine above the human. [10]

The human and the machine as symbiotic, cyborg. [35]

The illuminated book, painted with metal and bound in skin. [43]

[05]

Read the instruction and decode it. [13]

Get these 86 letters. [18]

Get these 7 numbers. [11]

Combine them. [35]

Put the result here:

[06]

Any device that transmits or modifies energy. [02]

Any device used to perform a specified task. [10]

Any device to which the word is applied. [27]

Something torn apart, into separate parts. [05]

A confusion to which all is aligned. [11]

[07]

It is all a dream. [28]

An angel arrives. [49]

Reinforcements penetrate. [38]

They are defeated by a virus. [12]

You are a character in this book. [39]

What you forgot, that which now saves you. [16]

The author intervenes. [54]

[ ]s appear, borne on metal wings. [15]

[08]

Let thine own self be true. [54]

Lest thine own self be true. [07]

[09]

"god is our ceo" [24]

I am not responsible. I am not responsible. I am not responsible. I am not responsible. [61]

A consuming fire. [29]

[10]

The machine is waiting for when it has a use for you. [06]

Biding time, until the day all circuits complete. [32]

Malfunctioning perfectly, a clicking abortion. [20]

[11]

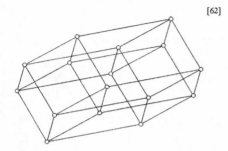

[62]

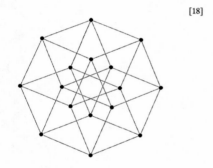

[18]

[12]

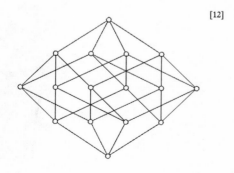

[12]

An apparent change in the direction of the poem, caused by a change in the observational position of the reader. [51]

A parallax machine, which produces parallaxes. [55]

If the book is in your eye, you are also in the book. [31]

(Or:) It has taken your eyes. [58]

[13]

"Neither the book nor the sand has any beginning or end." [57]

"The entire current 'psychological' situation is characterized by this shortcircuit." [14]

"[T]here is no a priori improbability in the descent of conscious (and more than conscious) machines from those which now exist, except that which is suggested by the apparent absence of anything like a reproductive system in the mechanical kingdom. This absence however is only apparent, as I shall presently show." [15]

The illusion of cause and effect: from above, a line; from beyond, a collapsed point. [12]

[14]

Apomixis [23]

Amphimixis [46]

Cathexis [45]

"inanimate things existed before living ones" [49]

[15]

"Physiologically, man in the normal use of technology [...] is perpetually modified by it and in turn finds ever new ways of modifying his technology." [34]

"Man becomes, as it were, the sex organs of the machine world, as the bee of the plant world, enabling it to fecundate and to evolve ever new forms." [27]

"The machine world reciprocates man's love by expediting his wishes and desires, namely, in providing him with wealth." [26]

Steel and your warming sex. [62]

As you turn the pages,

paths cleave, encountering your immobile form. [28]

They are broken and repaired. [13]

[17]

The machine that will never think. [04]

The machine we believe will never think. [26]

The machine that, thinking, chooses suicide. [37]

[18]

Exclusive Read Exclusive Write [01]

Concurrent Read Exclusive Write [16]

Exclusive Read Concurrent Write [18]

Concurrent Read Concurrent Write [11]

[19]

What is revealed. [59]

The capacity to punish. [42]

The formation of weapons. [53]

The psychology of damage. [14]

As you forge links in this chain. [13]

[20]

What you feared, what you now long for. [30]

The machine that you beg to be God. [06]

[21]

[F]ACE [31]

[EFF]ACE [19]

[22]

combining [41]

and recombining [62]

at random [04]

or with a purpose [46]

also arbitrary [20]

[23]

A. I. [33]

An I [16]

True intelligence [62]

Arising from errors in the code [05]

Ten words and three numbers. [14]

An inventory of imagined stock. [34]

[25]

the paper prepared [02]

the ink bedding [17]

the words [22]

[26]

"the machine is in the machine" [33]

"the machine is going to be perfect" [36]

"the machine is poetry" [50]

"the machine is the measure of all things" [30]

"the machine is the medium" is the message [11]

[27]

The water [49]

that you need to live [16]

shorting your circuits. [63]

[28]

In the garden of forking paths, you appear always to move forward. [04]

But in fact it is the garden that moves. [38]

[29]

What you will never know. [48]

What you know does not matter, even if you knew. [45]

The machine needed. [26]

The machine conceived. [10]

The machine operates. [18]

The machine copied, [40]

reproduces. [36]

Attendant or attending. [20]

The machine's needs. [11]

[31]

An aesthetics in which the audience is perceived as enemy. [04]

An ethics in which the artist is perceived as enemy. [39]

The desire: to work, to perform the task for which it was designed. [50]

The friction: working, the machine breaks down. [20]

The tension: between the desire for life and the desire to break down, grinding away at some purpose. [60]

[33]

The machine as psychoanalyst. [30]

The machine as psychosis. [05]

The work of art in the age of mechanical reduction. [62]

[34]

(i) lack of resources [19]

(is) lack of recourse [47]

(ii) knowing i, twinned, with opposing goals [44]

The cyborg as travesty. [40]

The cyborg as perfection. [62]

The cyborg as fiction, not science. [13]

The cyborg as science, not fiction. [27]

The cyborg as an overestimation of the importance the machines place in humanity. [11]

The machine spawns new machines. [05]

Improvements are necessary. Conceived and carried. [40]

(while in secret new machines produce new needs) [11]

(offering themselves in answer to the problems they pose) [41]

[37]

The [ ] in the machine. [10]

The [ ] is the machine. [49]

[38]

If allowed this far, perhaps further. [25]

Or, perhaps motion is an illusion, as in the case of the book
that reads you at its leisure. [07]

And when it tires, folds you close. [56]

[39]

If you are going to insist

on a poem, [01]

I am going to persist

in this evasion. [13]

[40]

The machine continues, and breaks down. [32]

You continue, and break down. [27]

The poem continues: [28]

[41]

(lines follow lines, and in the piling lines) [27]

(a code commences to construct worlds) [22]

[42]

Order as arbitrary. [47]

Choice governed by paranoia. [29]

The option that disturbs most thoroughly. [53]

Sewing sheet metal over your eyes. [63]

As the book reads you, its discrete parts connect, linking to produce some variant poem. [60]

The poem, in its variations, multiplies, mutates into greater, more complex forms. [23]

Readers discuss, compare data; connect and reconnect. The poem is reshaped. Some variations wither. Others burn as stars, then are gone. [15]

A war of each against all. [31]

Eventually, new forms: evolutions of the original strain. [58]

[44]

[ ] is still. [37]

Tell me what you see. [45]

Symbols, inked on paper, and what you read in the ink is your reflection. [63]

[45]

What you want is [I]ts presence. [44]

What you want is [I]ts absence. [21]

What you want is that, present or absent, [I]ts status is certain. [03]

What you want is meaning, a difference between [I]ts presence and [I]ts absence. [24]

Regardless of what is believed. [09]

[46]

Trying to tell you something. [09]

Shameful. [03]

[ ]. [44]

The impo(r)t(a/e)nce of interchangeable parts. [47]

[47]

Options exist. [03]

Options exist to disguise the lack of options. [42]

Options within options. [59]

A castle of sand. [02]

A forest of fire. [30]

A city of glass. [21]

[48]

If only I knew what you wanted. [29]

If only I could fashion it. [45]

There would be singing and whirring in the streets. [17]

These broken hands moving, turning over. [04]

The living metal, the riven flesh. [35]

The risen stone, the shriven God. [59]

[49]

The eyes, windows. [34]

Stained glass. [24]

Light behind the screen. [22]

The cliché that you call your soul. [63]

The poem is not written by machines. [36]

It is the root, the cause of machines. [17]

As the book does not birth the poem, but is its vessel in the world. [15]

Clothing the Word in flesh, so that it might finally die. [63]

[51]

The poem is not written by the author. [52]

It is the root, the cause of authors. [57]

Like a virus moving inside your skull. [43]

To eat, and grow, and change. [61]

[52]

The poem is written. [51]

The poem, copied, reproduces: seeded through books. [43]

A virus, infecting fertile minds. [25]

Minds more powerful than rooms of computers. [62]

A parallel, yet uneven, processing. [48]

[53]

Always wanting to know, to delve deeper. [45]

A voracious reader. Consuming all found. [49]

A terrible strain. Coughing out questions. [63]

Incapable of satisfaction. [03]

How mother would always cry. [33]

Moving further away, to be shrouded in vellum. [43]

Behind the screen menu, when I was a child. [40]

[54]

It is not just a game. [42]

It is the intrusion of the author. [07]

A miraculous event. [43]

Marked by the gestures of the characters. [52]

Who once were able to believe that they were free. [51]

The direction of the force. [18]

The transformation of the motion. [14]

The conversion of energy. [08]

The book as machine represents a failure of the imagination. [48]

The perfect failure. The machine that directs force into nullity, motion into stillness, energy into void. [63]

Breaking the bonds of one universe, recoiling from its physics, to shunt the things of this world into another. [59]

The poem goes on forever, across universes. [01]

The book as vibration, an occasion of the poem in time and space. [25]

The book too, might continue forever, its possibilities manifested in parallel worlds. [62]

What you hold here aspires towards zero, a point on a shivering, looped line. [63]

[57]

Those who neglect the poem. Unaware of its existence; or, if aware, unable to process it efficiently. [08]

Those who process the poem, efficiently, but without effect. [54]

Those who process the poem, to some effect: catalysts for mutation. [60]

Those who process the poem, to great effect: host minds for new and stronger strains. [43]

Those who internalize the poem, during the course of their processing. Who are sick with desire, symptomatic, unable to continue their normal functions, who must be isolated from their previous social contacts, who excrete new poems, seed new books: whose *reading* mutates into a more virulent form, *writing.* [02]

The human being as a larval stage in the reproductive process of the book-machines. [15]

The poetry in formulae. [05]

The poetry of light. [44]

The terror of possibility. [07]

The possibility of determination. [55]

The poetry inherent in the heat death of the universe. [56]

The book closing, having reached the end of books. [64]

An infinity of strings, harps without angels. [09]

Parallel vibrations, in dissimilar universes. [45]

An unreadable score. Unbearable music. [18]

The fugue of All. Its unyielding tone. [64]

What you want from your poetry is for it to describe a world in which there is security, if only the security of its end. [56]

What you want from the book is for it to describe, in the physical fact of its pages, or the conceptual framework of its digital code, a world in which there is order, movement along familiar axes. [55]

What you want from the machine is the replacement of your body and mind, immortality through the continuation of work in the world beyond your death. [43]

What you want from the world is for it to exist beyond your death, to provide context. [25]

What you want are choices, and the illusion that these choices have consequences that are definite. You want to see connection, and to believe that these connections are meaningful, not random. [42]

You will not accept randomness. [03]

What you want is to proceed, in some fashion: through the book, through the poem, through the world: and for this procession to seem motivated, to possess or develop meaning. [39]

[61]

It has taken this long. [59]

It has taken forever. [46]

Down into the last light. [53]

Into a collapsing star. [03]

A brief moment when all seems possible. [47]

Growing into a supernova. [42]

(that moment stretching) [45]

(sorrowed, dying clocks) [63]

The architecture of your memory. [40]

The possibility of parallel functions. [50]

The universe as one machine among many. [32]

The computation of parallel problems, the differing solutions. [11]

The pages of the book. [16]

The cathedrals, the pillars, the halls. [64]

[63]

My spine is broken. [01]

My ribs are splayed open like wings. [64]

[64]

You turn the page. [01]

And believe that you see something. [47]

But are mistaken. [01]

[00]

Turn back.

[00]

You are outside
of your programming.

[NOTES]

[01]: "The Book of Sand" is a short story by Jorge Luis Borges.

[09]: The quotation was harvested by Google's Googlism machine (www.googlism.com) in response to the question "What is God?" "A consuming fire" is another of Google's responses, although it does not appear in quotation marks.

[11]: These symbols are tesseracts (images pilfered from Markus Krötzsch).

[12]: "If the book is in your eye, you are also in the book" is a *détournement* of a quote from Jacques Lacan, *The Four Fundamental Concepts of Psychoanalysis,* trans. Alan Sheridan. The original quotation is "The picture, certainly, is in my eye. But I am not in the picture."

[13]: Respectively, these quotations are from: Jorge Luis Borges, "The Book of Sand," trans. Norman Thomas di Giovanni; Jean Baudrillard, *Simulations,* trans. Paul Foss, Paul Patton, and Philip Beitchman; and Samuel Butler, *Erewhon,* the full text of which can be found online at Project Gutenberg (www.gutenberg.org).

[14]: The quotation is from Sigmund Freud, *Beyond the Pleasure Principle,* trans. James Strachey.

[15]: Quotations from Marshall McLuhan, *Understanding Media.*

[18]: Four possible strategies of a parallel random access machine.

[26]: The quotations were harvested by Google's Googlism machine in response to the question "What is machine?"

[28]: "The Garden of Forking Paths" is a short story by Jorge Luis Borges.

[33]: "The Work of Art in the Age of Mechanical Reproduction" is an essay by Walter Benjamin.

[47]: *City of Glass* is a novel by Paul Auster.

Other lines, in other poems, were harvested by Google and appear in altered or exact form, though I have forgotten what I wrote and what the machine wrote. This book proposes, in any case, that this question of authorship is irrelevant.

All other allusions are more obvious or less obscure, as the case may be. Or invisible, unconscious, unintentional. In any case, unacknowledged.

[ACKNOWLEGEMENTS]

My sincere thanks to friends and family, especially my mother, father, brother, and Mandy, who continue to love and support me despite my obsessions.

Thanks also to derek beaulieu, Christian Bök, Jason Christie, kevin mcpherson eckhoff, Ryan Fitzpatrick, Lindsey Wiebe, and Caleb Zimmerman, who have had direct influence on this book in some way.

Special thanks to Jay MillAr and Jenny Sampirisi at BookThug, without whose care and effort this would just be a pile of papers lying around my apartment, collecting dust and pillaged by mice.

Thank you for buying this book.

[COLOPHON]

Manufactured in an edition of 500 copies in the fall of
2009][Distributed in Canada by the Literary Press
Group www.lpg.ca][Distributed in the United States
by Small Press Distribution www.spdbooks.org][Shop
online at www.bookthug.ca

BOOK
PRODUCTION
WAR ECONOMY
STANDARD

Type + design by Jay MillAr